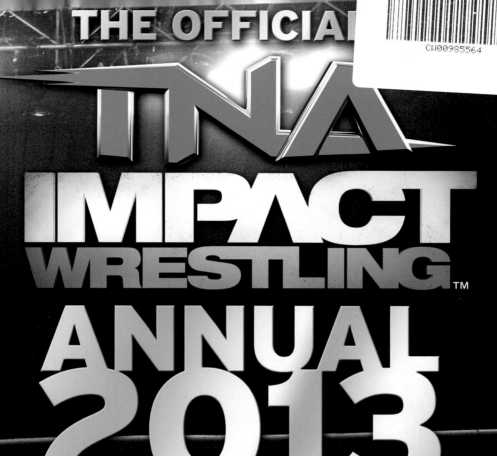

THE OFFICIAL TNA IMPACT WRESTLING™ ANNUAL 2013

Written by Matthew J. Hardy

Designed by Jon Dalrymple

A Grange Publication

© 2012. Published by Grange Communications Ltd., Edinburgh, under licence from TNA Impact Wrestling. Printed in the EU.

ISBN: 978-1-908925-21-3

CONTENTS

GUESS WHO?

TNA WORLD HEAVYWEIGHT CHAMPION

TNA TV CHAMPIONSHIP

TNA KNOCKOUTS TA

TNA X DIVISION CHAMPIONSHIP

Can you work out wh
behind the cham
answers in the bla
your answers at th

TNA TAG TEAM CHAMPIONSHIPS

A Ω

...EAM CHAMPIONSHIPS

TNA KNOCKOUTS CHAMPIONSHIP

TNA wrestlers are hidden
...nship belts? Write your
...spaces, and then check
...ack of this book (P60-61).

BOBBY

After winning the 12-man Bound for Glory Series for a shot at the TNA World Heavyweight Championship, Bobby Roode finally got his chance to shine against then-champion Kurt Angle. However, despite having the momentum and fan support behind him, Roode came up short against the former Olympian. He wasn't the first and won't be the last. However, when his Beer Money partner James Storm shocked the world the following week and did what Bobby Roode could not – beat Angle for the title – Roode snapped, and his jealous nature took hold. The friendly rivalry between the partners turned bitter during their first World Title match on the Nov 3rd 2011 edition of Impact Wrestling, where Bobby Roode hit Storm over the head with his own trademark beer bottle, cheating his way to victory and his first TNA World Heavyweight Championship.

ROODE

(BOBBY ROODE)

HEIGHT: 6'0"
WEIGHT: 240LBS
FROM: TORONTO, CANADA
FINISHING MOVE: THE PAY OFF

It was the bottle-shot heard around the world, which spelled not only the end of a friendship, but the end of one of the greatest tag teams in TNA history. Beer Money was no more.

Heading into disputes with AJ Styles, Jeff Hardy and the 'Insane Icon' Sting, which all led to successful World title defences, Roode quickly established a name for himself as a champion who would do whatever it took to keep hold of his precious championship. Roode was a man not afraid to cheat to win.

But since winning the gold, Bobby Roode and his former best friend had been on a collision course. Somehow, they kept apart until Lockdown in April 2012.

FUN FACT: Bobby Roode made his wrestling debut in 1998 under the moniker 'Total' Lee Awesome. Probably the biggest rise to superstardom over the last 12 months has been that of former multiple time tag team champion Bobby Roode. Many had predicted great things for Bobby Roode, but this was finally the year that he struck gold as a singles star.

The heated battle for the title commenced outside of the 15-foot steel cage with both men trading blows back and forth. Once entering the cage, it was Storm who looked in control of the match in front of his hometown fans. At the conclusion of the epic battle, however, with both competitors wearing a crimson mask, it was Bobby Roode, who once again came out on top after falling through the open cage door and out to the floor following a James Storm Superkick, thus winning the match. Though some might consider Roode to have been fortunate in this and other title defences, no one can argue that this guy is the real deal.

Bobby Roode cemented his legacy when he became the longest-reigning TNA World Heavyweight Champion of all time by surpassing the 211-day record set by TNA Original AJ Styles. There is no doubt that TNA and the wrestling world have had a 'Roode' awakening.

SLAMMIVERSARY

TNA UK T

The relationship between TNA and its UK fans is as strong as any. Having long supported TNA from a distance, in the last few years, UK fans have been treated to exhilarating live performances from their favourite TNA superstars on home soil up and down the country.

Capitalising on their runaway UK success in 2011, TNA came back across the pond in January 2012 for another sell-out arena tour. On this, TNA's fourth trip to the UK, the 'Maximum Impact Tour' hit Dublin, Glasgow, Nottingham and Manchester, before ending their run at the historic Wembley Arena in London before a jam-packed crowd of 5,500 screaming fans.

On that extra special night in Wembley, for the first time ever, TNA thanked the UK fans for their continued support by recording two episodes of their smash hit, flagship TV show, Impact Wrestling. The shows would be seen worldwide, demonstrating the reach of TNA. All the stars were out, and UK fans saw legends like Hulk Hogan and Sting cross the Atlantic for the first time in decades along with the young and dynamic stars of TNA's present and future.

As TNA's fan base in the UK grows, the more fans become passionate for more non-stop action. And TNA will be back again in January 2013 for more international Impacts. Check out the advert on page 15 for all the details of where you can see TNA Impact Wrestling in 2013.

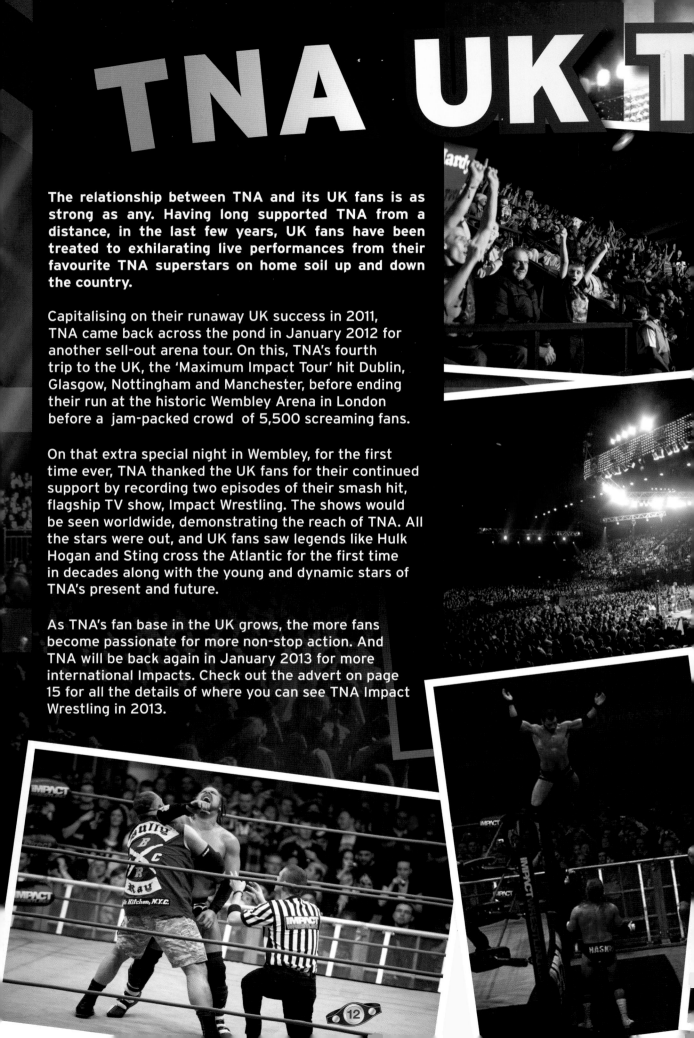

12

DOUGLAS WILLIAMS

🐦 @DougWilliamsUK)

Douglas Williams is a British Wrestling legend and has been a star in Britain for almost 20 years. Trained by the NWA Hammerlock team, Doug is one of the most technically sound wrestlers in the world. To see Douglas Williams wrestle a match, using the tightest chain wrestling, is a joy to behold, and fans are treated to an innovative and unique British style that is a long-forgotten art in many corners of wrestling. As a former tag team champion and X-Division champion in TNA, Douglas Williams still has one dream left – to be TNA World Heavyweight Champion. Williams definitely has the talent for one run at the top prize. Whatever is in Doug Williams' future, we can thank him for opening the doors for British talent in TNA. The British invasion has begun.

HEIGHT: 5'10"
WEIGHT: 225LBS
FROM: READING, ENGLAND
FINISHING MOVE: THE CHAOS THEORY

WINTER

🐦 @infamous_winter)

Despite being the only Brit to capture the TNA Knockouts Championship, Winter has been an enigma of sorts. With her mix of technical prowess and aerial ability, the enchanting temptress has cast her spell over many in the Knockouts division, but none more so than Angelina Love. The duo share a unique bond which perhaps only they can explain. Winter became consort to Angelina, dealing out advice and friendship to her new partner in crime. Together they became a formidable and powerful team that held the Knockouts Tag Team titles. What more does this British beauty have up her sleeve, and is there more gold in her future?

14

WRESTLING

ROAD TO
LOCK DOWN
TOUR

2013 MAXIMUM IMPACT V

AUSTIN ARIES   KURT ANGLE   JEFF HARDY

AJ STYLES - BOBBY ROODE - MR. ANDERSON - ROB VAN DAM
JAMES STORM - GAIL KIM - MISS TESSMACHER - MAGNUS
CHRISTOPHER DANIELS & KAZARIAN - PLUS MANY MORE TBA!

JANUARY 2013

MON	21	**DUBLIN NATIONAL STADIUM**	0818 719 300
WED	23	**GLASGOW BRAEHEAD ARENA**	0844 499 9990
THU	24	**NOTTINGHAM ARENA**	0844 412 4624
FRI	25	**MANCHESTER ARENA**	0844 847 8000
SAT	26	**LONDON WEMBLEY ARENA**	0844 815 0815

★ GIGSANDTOURS.COM 0844 811 0051 ★ TICKETMASTER.CO.UK 0844 826 2826 ★

f TNAWRESTLINGUK    IMPACTWRESTLING.com    CHALLENGE TNA EUROSTORE

★ ONE CAGE MATCH PER EVENT   CARD SUBJECT TO CHANGE

Spot the Difference

USE YOUR SKILL AND JUDGEMENT TO SPOT THE 12 DIFFERENCES BETWEEN THESE TWO PICTURES. THEN, CHECK YOUR ANSWERS ON P60.

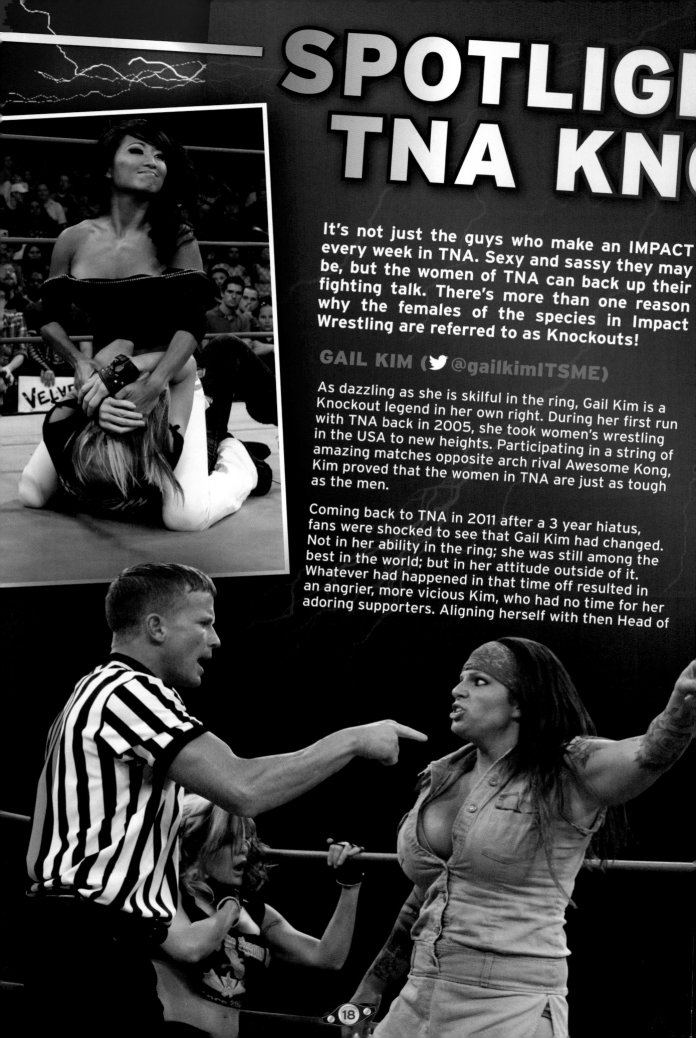

It's not just the guys who make an IMPACT every week in TNA. Sexy and sassy they may be, but the women of TNA can back up their fighting talk. There's more than one reason why the females of the species in Impact Wrestling are referred to as Knockouts!

GAIL KIM (@gailkimITSME)

As dazzling as she is skilful in the ring, Gail Kim is a Knockout legend in her own right. During her first run with TNA back in 2005, she took women's wrestling in the USA to new heights. Participating in a string of amazing matches opposite arch rival Awesome Kong, Kim proved that the women in TNA are just as tough as the men.

Coming back to TNA in 2011 after a 3 year hiatus, fans were shocked to see that Gail Kim had changed. Not in her ability in the ring; she was still among the best in the world; but in her attitude outside of it. Whatever had happened in that time off resulted in an angrier, more vicious Kim, who had no time for her adoring supporters. Aligning herself with then Head of the Knockouts division, Karen Jarrett, and Madison Rayne quickly delivered benefits however. Within a month, Gail Kim was holder of both the TNA Knockouts Tag Team titles (with Rayne) and the coveted Knockouts Championship. Though she lost the tag straps to ODB and Eric Young, Kim continued to gain plaudits by successfully defending her singles gold against any and all opponents including Mickie James, Velvet Sky, Tara, Miss Tessmacher, and even ally, Madison Rayne. She became one of several TNA stars to break records in 2012 by becoming the longest-reigning Knockouts Champion in history.

ODB (🐦 @TheODBBAM)

ODB is a rough, smash-mouth competitor, who relies more on brawn than finesse but still has the great wrestling skills in the ring to school her opponents. This former 3-time TNA Knockout Champion is perhaps the toughest of all the TNA women. You're more likely to find ODB, or 'One Dirty B*tch' – to give her her full name – drinking in the bar than modelling with the rest of the TNA Knockouts. Certainly ODB is one gal who doesn't clamour for attention. What you see is what you get with ODB. However, that's not to say ODB can't be wooed. She may be a little unorthodox, but then that is perhaps why she found love with equally cooky Eric Young. The pair not only tied the knot in 2012 but also – in an equally unlikely scenario – captured the TNA Knockouts Tag Team titles from Gail Kim and Madison Rayne. The match made in heaven inside and outside the ring, should continue to go from strength to strength.

MISS TESSMACHER
(🐦 @BrookeTess)

Miss Tessmacher certainly lives up to the name Knockout. Having won over 20 beauty pageant titles in her life, some doubted whether she had the in-ring ability to go with her stunning looks.

SPOTLIGHT ON THE TNA KNOCKOUTS

MICKIE JAMES (🐦 @MickieJames)

Since returning to TNA in 2010, Mickie James has always been a crowd favourite. Years of dedication to her craft has won her a legion of fans and made her one of the biggest names in women's wrestling over the last decade. Though Mickie James had won countless titles in her career, her goal from day one in TNA was to become Knockouts champion. She reached her holy grail at Lockdown 2011 by defeating Madison Rayne in just a minute during a memorable cage match as the fans cheered on. Mickie James had an impressive four-month reign, but her goal since then, and going forward, is to recapture the Knockouts title for a second time.

Away from the Impact Zone, Mickie James has highlighted her extraordinary talents by pursuing a music career. In 2010 she released her first country music album, 'Strangers and Angels', to critical acclaim and plans to release her eagerly anticipated follow-up album in 2012.

BROOKE HOGAN (🐦 @MizzHogan)

'Whatcha gonna do, brother?' Hang on a minute, there's another Hogan running wild in TNA. Daughter of the legendary Hulk Hogan, Brooke has made a name for herself as a global TV personality and musician, but in June 2012 she added another string to her bow, joining her dad in the world of professional wrestling and TNA Wrestling. Not content to just sit around, Brooke debuted as the new executive in charge of the Knockouts division with the role of elevating the profile of the TNA women. An instant hit with the Impact Zone audience, this beautiful blonde proved she 'ain't the lady to mess with'.

The redhead may officially be retired from the ring as a wrestler, but she still kicks butt in the backstage area. Making the smooth transition to backstage interviewer was no easy feat. However, her fun-loving attitude and easy-going style makes her a hit with wrestlers and fans alike. And Christy's connection with the fans has drawn her out from the back to become the lead ring announcer in TNA. When fans hear Christy's voice, they know to get ready to rumble.

TARA (@TARALiSAMARiE)

Tara is a mean girl with a vicious streak when she wants to be. It is that personality trait which has led her to four Knockouts titles and a Knockouts tag team title. A legend in North American women's wrestling, Tara is now the true test of any Knockout vying for a place on the roster as newcomer Taeler Hendrix found out during her 'Gut Check Challenge' on Impact Wrestling. Acting as mentor to Miss Tessmacher, when they formed the successful 'TnT' tandem that won tag gold, Tara passed on her years of knowledge to her younger partner, which no doubt enriched Miss Tessmacher with that extra skill to enable her to win her own singles Knockout title.

MADISON RAYNE (@MRayneTNA)

It seems Angelina Love wasn't the only former member of the Beautiful People to discover there is safety in numbers. Though a much celebrated singles wrestler with a technical attack, Madison Rayne soon found a home as part of the power trio with Gail Kim and Karen Jarrett. As a result of the alliance, Madison Rayne has been almost untouchable in recent times. Rayne has made a habit of getting involved in matches to help Kim retain her championship, though that's not to say Madison Rayne doesn't have her own aspirations for the title. In March 2012, she and Kim clashed for the Knockouts title shortly after they lost the tag straps to ODB and Eric Young. Whilst the friendship seemed on the rocks, in defeat, Madison Rayne and Kim ultimately grew stronger. That can only spell trouble for the rest of the Knockouts locker room.

TNA CROSSWORD

Answers on p60-61.

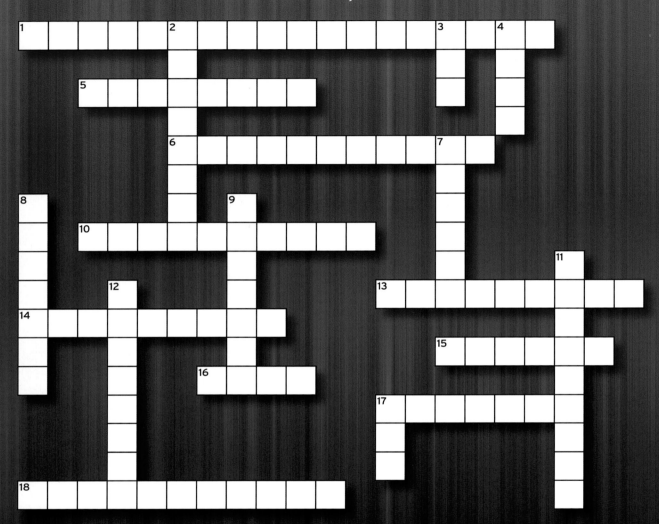

ACROSS

1 The only two TNA Originals to be with the company throughout. (2,6 & 5,5)
5 A chance for independent stars to win TNA contracts. (3,5)
6 President of TNA Wrestling. (5,6)
10 The self-proclaimed '@$$hole'. (2,8)
13 The UK TV channel which airs TNA. (9)
14 Stable led by Hulk Hogan. (9)
15 _____ Wrestling, TNA's flagship show. (6)
16 Fireworks are also known as these, which kick off TNA PPVs. (4)
17 City where TNA's show comes from most weeks, _____, Florida. (7)
18 X-Division star whose name forms part of the Zodiac. (6,5)

DOWN

2 PPV that sounds like a prison scenario. (8)
3 Mike Tenay's co-commentator. (3)
4 ____ Ka King, TNA's sister promotion in India. (4)
7 'The Charismatic _____'. Nickname of Jeff Hardy. (6)
8 What a wrestler does when he cannot stand the pain any more. (7)
9 The London Arena where TNA attracted their biggest crowd. (7)
11 The women of TNA. (9)
12 If you're outside the ring for too long, the result is a _____. (8)
17 Female wrestler who married Eric Young in 2012. (3)

STARS OF THE IMPACT ZONE WORDSEARCH

Can you find the 18 stars of TNA Impact Wrestling hidden in the wordsearch grid below? Answers on p60-61. Words can go horizontally, vertically and diagonally in all eight directions.

```
X Y Y K N O S R E D N A R M M
N D J L A K B K S T I N G W M
S R A Q Q Z A K R O B B I E E
E A M Q E B A M I K L I A G R
M H E T Y L F R R N H T G M R
A F S S Y N G L I U T R J E G
J F S S T K M N L A X C D N A
E E T W A B S K A K N O R H J
I J O W F M H T S T O Y R T S
K R R K F O O U E R R M M Z T
C E M J G J N A Y V X U K L Y
I T Q A T G P B J T L C K Z L
M N N X A G B H F O M E N K E
Q I N M R O L D Y N E W V N S
Z W P Q B B U L L Y R A Y W M
```

Abyss	JamesStorm	MrAnderson
AJStyles	JeffHardy	RobbieE
BobbyRoode	Kazarian	SamoaJoe
BullyRay	KurtAngle	Sting
GailKim	Magnus	VelvetSky
HulkHogan	MickieJames	Winter

23

JEFF

(🐦 @ JEF

After one of the toughest years the North Carolina native has ever endured personally and professionally, Jeff Hardy returned to Impact wrestling in August 2011 a changed man. Gone were the frailties of his past that had led him off the path to prominence. In a heartfelt apology to the fans he had let down months earlier by putting on a disappointing performance versus Sting, the 'Charismatic Enigma' asked for his followers to forgive him. In return, he promised to come back faster, stronger, and better than ever.

Jeff didn't let anyone down. Back on the trail of the TNA World title, Jeff Hardy has had to earn his way back to the top. Never more than a Swanton away from victory, Jeff battled champion Bobby Roode in a heated match at Turning Point 2012 but came up short due to Roode's cheating tactics. Jeff never received a fair one-on-one rematch; constant interference on more than one occasion saw to that. But, this led Jeff Hardy towards a dream feud. Through spring 2012, Hardy and former multiple-time World champion, Kurt Angle battled on every big stage. Whilst trading victories over the series of matches, it was Jeff Hardy who eventually earned his opponent's respect, winning their final encounter inside the Lockdown cage following a jaw-dropping Swanton from the top of the structure.

A former TNA World Champion and leader of a generation of wrestling fans, the high-flying, death-defying 'rock star' of pro wrestling, is back to his best. Constantly pushing the boundaries of what the human body can endure

FUN FACT: Jeff Hardy first appeared in TNA June 23, 2004.

HARDY

(HARDYBRAND)

and what is possible in wrestling, Jeff Hardy takes life to the extreme. Though never the biggest, you can never count Jeff Hardy out. His biggest strength is his heart; a heart that won't let him quit; a heart that means a legion of fans' cheers for the 'Charismatic Enigma'.

HEIGHT: 6'2"
WEIGHT: 215LBS
FROM: CAMERON, NORTH CAROLINA
FINISHING MOVE: THE SWANTON

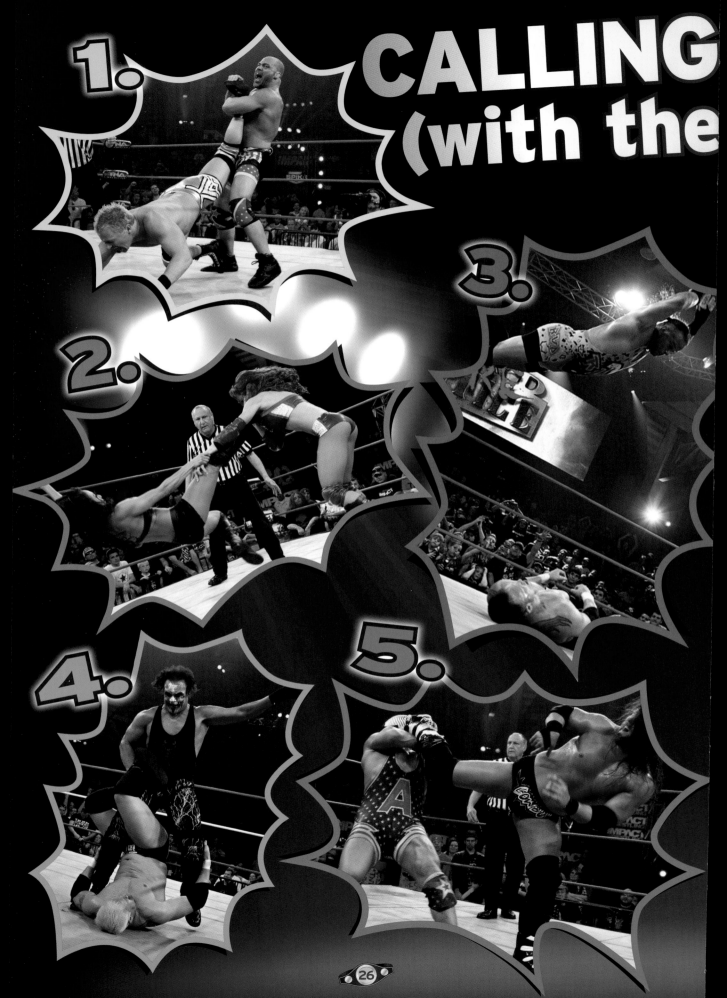

THE MOVES
(Professor)

Mike Tenay (🐦 @REALMikeTenay) has been calling the action in TNA since the very beginning, but can you name the moves being performed in the pictures below by TNA Superstars? Put your answers in the spaces provided, and then check if you're correct on pages 60-61.

6.

1. ....
2. ....
3. ....
4. ....
5. ....
6. ....
7. ....
8. ....

7.

8.

G.CO.

EPIC
#1 Samoa Joe vs. Kurt Angle

The origins of the most commercially successful feud in TNA history dates back to 2006 when Kurt Angle debuted in TNA. At the time, Samoa Joe had taken the TNA Heavyweight title hostage and refused to return it for the then-champion Jeff Jarrett's upcoming title defence against Sting at Bound for Glory. With Samoa Joe ignoring threats of contract termination by TNA commissioner Jim Cornette, Kurt Angle took matters into his own hands. Having been made the special enforcer of the Jarrett-Sting match, Angle interrupted Joe and head-butted his foe between the eyes. As a fight ensued, Jarrett was able to snatch back the title belt, but a line had been drawn between the young pretender and the Olympic master. Whilst it was Angle who won these early collisions, ending the 'Samoan Submission Machine's 18-month undefeated streak, the two would be constantly drawn together for the next two years. It was at Lockdown 2008, where the epic feud reached its peak.

Inside the 15-foot cage, the world champion Kurt Angle and Samoa Joe went to war. The physicality and the emotion on this night surpassed all their previous amazing matches. On this night, with Joe's career on the line as well as the title, Samoa Joe and Kurt Angle produced one of the most talked about matches of the decade. Presented as an MMA-style wrestling match, it helped Lockdown 2008 break TNA PPV records and became the most-watched PPV match in TNA history, ending with Samoa Joe delivering the 'Muscle Buster' to his opponent to win his first TNA World Heavyweight Championship.

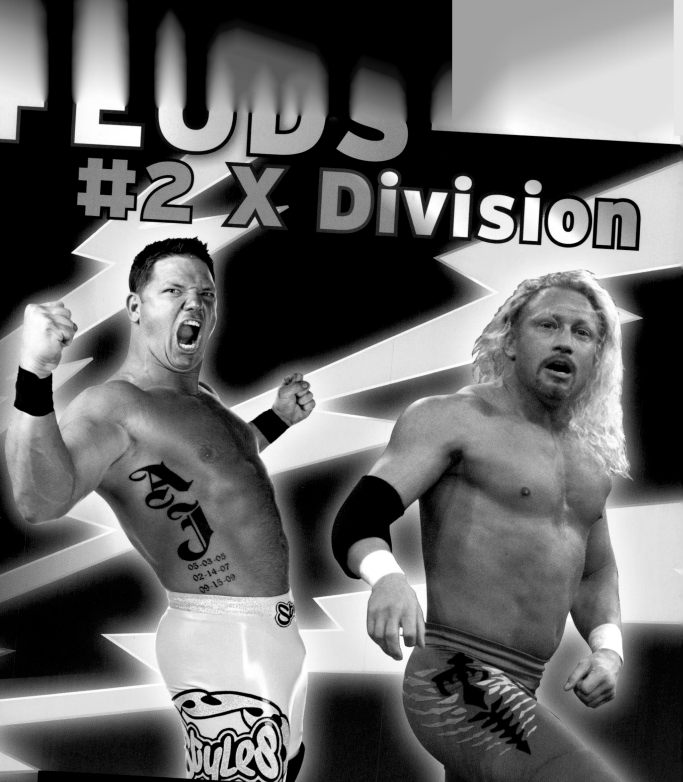

FEUDS
#2 X Division

Throughout the early days of TNA's weekly programme, there was one thing that the wrestling world was talking about, the X Division. And though many X Division stars passed through the Asylum, it was the feud between the relatively unknown AJ Styles and the veteran Jerry Lynn, which had people coming back for more. No matter how many times the two faced off, be it in singles, tag, triple-threat, cage or ladder matches; fans knew to expect a classic. The high-flying, outrageous, never-before-seen moves of the young AJ Styles, versus the tactical and technical mastery of Jerry Lynn, were must-see TV and made sure all eyes were glued to TNA Wrestling. It was one of the key rivalries to put TNA on the map. Throughout TNA history, AJ Styles is a constant thread for classic matches from the X Division that made the championship at times, even more revered in the fans eyes, than the world title.

EPIC FEUDS
#3 Gail Kim vs. Awesome Kong

On October 17, 2007, Gail Kim won a 10-women gauntlet match to officially become TNA's first-ever Knockout champion. Though the creation of the title was a reward for the female stars doing such great work in TNA, for Kim, it was the culmination of a life's work. But it was not long before the dream became a nightmare as Gail Kim was faced with a new terrifying challenger in the form of Awesome Kong, a women twice Kim's size. Billed at 272 pounds and with an imposing reputation from Japan, Kong was something unique in women's wrestling. Clashing for the first time at Turning Point, the two women put on an amazing display, of heart by Gail Kim and of brutality by Awesome Kong. In a classic David vs. Goliath match, Kim somehow walked out with the title but only because Awesome Kong had been disqualified. In the no-DQ rematch the following month, Gail Kim would not be so fortunate. Kong became the most dominant force perhaps in all of TNA, winning the Knockouts Championship. But more than the wins or losses, the quality of the series of matches presented between Gail Kim and Awesome Kong were better than any women's match in the US in the last decade and fans tuned in en masse to watch. Kong vs. Kim will long be remembered as one of the greatest and most significant feuds ever and TNA was the better for it.

TEN-YEA

1 WHAT IS THE NICKNAME GIVEN TO TENNESEE STATE FAIRGROUNDS ARENA WHERE TNA HELD ALL OF THEIR PPV SHOWS FROM JULY 2002-JUNE 2004?

2 WHO WAS THE FIRST (NWA) WORLD HEAVYWEIGHT CHAMPION CROWNED ON THE FIRST SHOW IN 2002?

3 WHO DEFEATED KURT ANGLE AT LOCKDOWN 2008 TO CAPTURE HIS FIRST TNA WORLD HEAVYWEIGHT CHAMPIONSHIP?

4 WHERE DID TNA HOLD ITS FIRST IMPACT WRESTLING TAPING OUTSIDE OF THE USA IN 2012?

5 WHICH THREE SUPERSTARS OF PRO WRESTLING MADE THEIR TNA DEBUTS ON THE JANUARY 4, 2010 EPISODE OF iMPACT BECOMING MAINSTAYS ON THE ROSTER?

6 HOW MANY TIMES HAS BEER MONEY INC. WON THE TNA WORLD TAG TEAM TITLES?

7 WHICH WRESTLING LEGEND WON THE KING OF THE MOUNTAIN MATCH AT SLAMMIVERSARY 2005, AND BY DOING SO WON HIS ONE AND ONLY NWA WORLD HEAVYWEIGHT TITLE?

8 WHAT IS TNA'S BIGGEST EVENT OF THE YEAR?

AR QUIZ

9 BEFORE TAZ, WHO WAS MIKE TENAY'S REGULAR BROADCAST COLLEAGUE FOR iMPACT!?

10 WHAT WAS THE NAME OF THE TAG TEAM CONSISTING OF JAMES STORM AND CHRIS HARRIS?

11 AJ STYLES IS A TRIPLE CROWN WINNER IN TNA, HAVING WON THE WORLD, X DIVISION AND TAG TEAM TITLES. CAN YOU NAME THE OTHER THREE MEN TO HAVE DONE SO?

12 ON WHICH CHANNEL DOES TNA IMPACT WRESTLING AIR IN THE UK?

13 AUSTIN ARIES PREVIOUSLY WRESTLED FOR TNA IN 2006 UNDER WHAT NAME?

14 WHO WERE RECOGNISED AS THE LAST NWA TAG TEAM CHAMPIONS IN TNA?

15 WHO FOUNDED TNA IN 2002?

QUIZ ANSWERS CAN BE FOUND ON PAGE 61.

STING

(🐦 @STING)

As the first inductee into the TNA Hall of Fame, Sting can rightly be considered a cornerstone of TNA and has earned the admiration and respect of the wrestling industry at large. He is called the 'Icon' because to millions, he IS an icon. But in 2011, Sting became somewhat of a riddle. The Stinger appeared to lose his mind and 'The Insane Icon' was born. Bearing the chaotic face paint of a villainous madman, Sting delved into his dark side and recreated himself as an unpredictable figure to fear. Or so we thought.

It transpired that Sting was playing prophet and warning us all of what was to come. As Sting acted as Dixie Carter's representative in her struggle for power of TNA with the villainous Hulk Hogan and evil Eric Bischoff, he met Hogan at Bound for Glory that year for control of TNA. It was winner takes all. Sting turned back the years to submit his long-time adversary with the 'Scorpion Death Lock' during the blockbuster match. As a show of gratitude by Dixie, Sting was subsequently put in charge of Impact Wrestling.

As the General Manager of Impact Wrestling, Sting found himself struggling to keep everything and everyone in check. Nobody said being the boss was going to be easy, but the Stinger's life was being made increasingly difficult by the TNA Champion Bobby Roode. Unhappy with the way the champ was cheating or fluking his way through title defences, Sting stepped into the ring to show his younger foe a thing or two. Unfortunately for the Icon, being GM meant he couldn't focus his efforts in the ring to muster victory, but it led to the realisation that Sting wanted to get back to doing what he was born to do be a wrestler full-time.

Sting is one legend who shows no signs of slowing. Without the restraints of being boss, there is no doubt Sting will be back on the World title trail. Could Sting go on to become a six-time TNA Champion? This writer, for one, would not back against him.

FUN FACT: Sting's career began in 1985, where he teamed with Jim Hellwig, who later found fame as the Ultimate Warrior.

HEIGHT: 6'2"
WEIGHT: 250LBS
ROM: VENICE BEACH, CALIFORNIA
HING MOVE: SCORPION DEATH LOCK

SAMOA JOE

The Samoan Submission Machine and former TNA World Heavyweight Champion, Samoa Joe, is a rare breed of wrestler. He doesn't have the body-builder physique or the witty charisma, but Joe has earned the respect and support of the TNA audience for his brute force and strong combative style. Joe is an angry man who loves nothing more than a good fight. Win, lose or draw, when you step in the ring with Samoa Joe, you leave knowing you've been in a war.

Magnus has developed into one of the most exciting wrestlers to come out of British Wrestling within the last decade. As part of the British Invasion, Magnus was a former multiple time tag team champion and had an ever-growing following on both sides of the Atlantic thanks to his hard hitting style. Learning all he could from the technically brilliant Doug Williams in that team, Magnus' progression has been evident for all to see.

SAMOA JOE
HEIGHT: 6'2"
WEIGHT: 280LBS
FROM: AMERICAN SAMOA
FINISHING MOVE: THE MUSCLE BUSTER

MAGNUS
HEIGHT: 6'3"
WEIGHT: 240LBS
FROM: KING'S LYNN, ENGLAND
FINISHING MOVE: THE TORMENTUM

& MAGNUS
@MAGNUSOFFICIAL)

In December 2011, Samoa Joe and Magnus formed an improbable team. Originally put together as part of the Wild Card tournament where partners were randomly assigned to each other, whilst most teams formed that night were a one-off deal, Joe and Magnus decided to stick together and vowed to make a mark in the TNA tag team ranks. Winning the Wild Card Tournament earned them a shot at the tag titles, and whilst they just came up short on their first attempt, Joe and Magnus regrouped and went on to capture the gold from Matt Morgan and Crimson. The team that many said would never work were now top dogs and ready for any challenge.

Time will tell whether the setback of losing the titles a few months later will halt their progress as a team, but either way, Samoa Joe and Magnus both seem to have the fire back in their eyes, which can only be a positive for TNA but a disturbing notion of things to come for the rest of the TNA locker room.

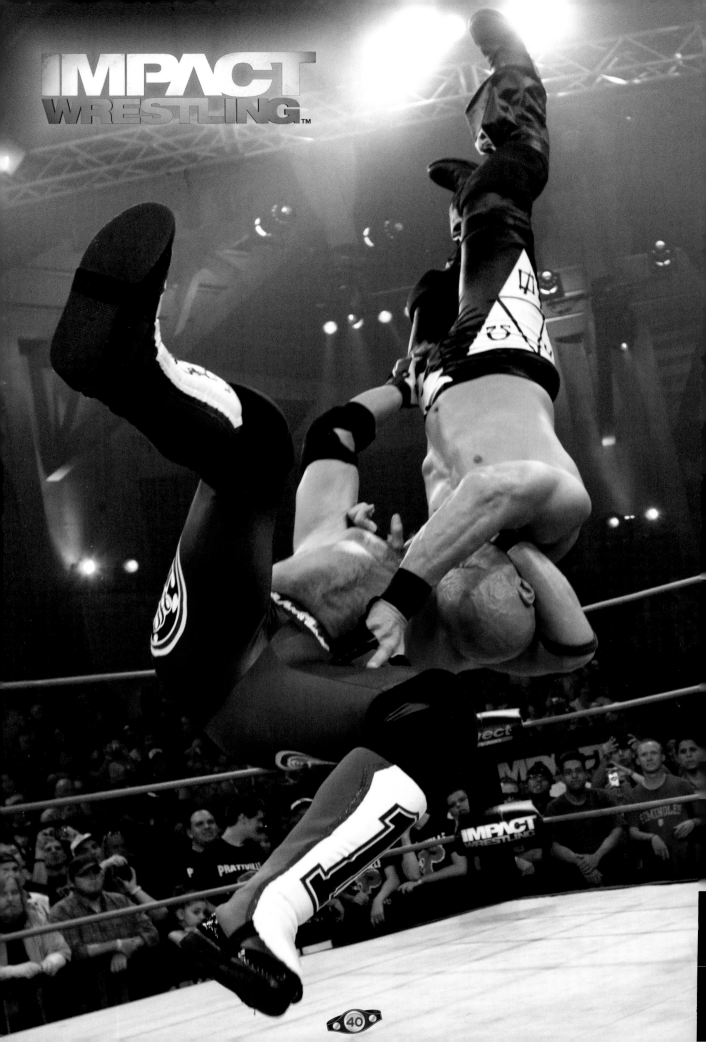

BOUND FOR GLORY MAZE

Help our heroic combatants find their way to the centre of the maze to see which two are gonna fight and be bound for glory! See page 61-62 for the answer.

BULLY

(🐦 @REAL

Once half of the most decorated tag team in all of professional wrestling history, Team 3D, with no less than 23 World Tag Team Titles from every major promotion across the globe (including three in TNA), when Brother Ray and Devon went their separate ways, a 'Bully' was born.

For the best part of 15 years, Bully Ray was seen as a tag-team wrestler. It can be one of the hardest taglines (no pun intended) to overcome. However, Ray has always been confident, but now a NEW confidence is evident. Some might say it's just his ego that has grown, but that aside, Bully Ray is now a major star on TNA Impact Wrestling and has gotten there by himself.

FUN FACT: Bully Ray is a fan of Italian Football.

5150

HARDCORE

GI✦FD

DOOM CREW INC.

Y RAY
(Bully 5150)

Never one to mince his words, Bully Ray has become renowned for his scathing verbal and physical attacks on wrestlers, announcers and fans. But it is in the ring where Bully Ray has made his biggest impact. Trading victories in intense blood feuds with former TNA World champions Mr. Anderson and James Storm in 2011-12, Bully Ray was closer than ever to his first World Heavyweight championship during this standout year. Ironically though, it may have been his close association with TNA champion Bobby Roode that has meant Bully Ray has not received the one-on-one title match he probably deserved.

Perhaps it was this frustration that led to Ray taking it out on the X Division. Bully, beware though. What goes around comes around, and those people he has stepped on during his rise to the top may one day come back to haunt him. Long-time fans will no doubt remember that Bully Ray was the last person to see Abyss at the Genesis PPV before the seven-foot monster vanished without trace. Will the monster return for revenge?

If Bully Ray continues into 2013 with the same momentum and aggression as he has done in 2012, then Bully Ray, TNA World Heavyweight Champion, may be the future for Impact Wrestling.

HEIGHT: 6'4"
WEIGHT: 326LBS
FROM: HELL'S KITCHEN, NEW YORK
FINISHING MOVE: THE BULLY BOMB

FINISH HIM WORDSEARCH

Can you find the 14 finishing moves of top TNA stars hidden in the grid below? Answers on page 60-61.

```
C N P C R E T S U B N I A R B
R M R P H L L P L U N G E R H
A B N E M A F L X F A G E N G
D L O M D Q O M A N H T K B H
L A T W X S G S G C S D M L S
E C N B X Q K L T U T O Y Y A
S K A F M L E Y B H B S V T L
H H W T Y S G E M Y E W A Z C
O O S N L K L Y L G L O F L S
C L X A C C R L G J D F R K E
K E M Y S J U S T R O K E Y L
M S F U T B T G H Y W Q Y D Y
Y L M T L G G K A K N Q R R T
M A Y X R P N P M M N M P N S
R M H G R M Z H X R J M D M C
```

Words can go horizontally, vertically and diagonally in all eight directions.

AngleSlam	**MuscleBuster**
BlackHoleSlam	**Payoff**
Brainbuster	**Plunge**
BullyBomb	**RedSky**
ChaosTheory	**Stroke**
Cradleshock	**StylesClash**
LastCall	**Swanton**

45

JAMES STORM

(@Cowboy_J_Storm)

Height: 6'0"
Weight: 240lbs
From:
Leipers Fork,
Tennessee
Finishing Move:
The Last Call

A firm fan favourite, James Storm's hard-hitting style has endeared him to audiences worldwide. The beer drinking, hell raiser James Storm has been a mainstay in TNA from the very first show. As a highly successful tag team wrestler, Storm has held the tag gold 11 times, as part of two of the greatest tag teams in TNA history, America's Most Wanted (with Chris Harris) and Beer Money Inc. (with Bobby Roode). But it is now in the singles ranks where James Storm belongs.

'Sorry about your damn luck'. The catchphrase made famous by 'The Cowboy'. Unfortunately, it became a phrase that would come back to bite him in the butt during his all-too-brief TNA World Title reign in October 2011. Just eight days after the TNA Original shocked the wrestling world to beat Kurt Angle for TNA's top prize, James Storm fell victim to a premeditated abuse of sportsmanship. Up against his best friend, then fellow Beer Money teammate, Bobby Roode, Storm had expected a clean match where the best man would win. Roode had other plans, and when things weren't going his way, he crashed a beer bottle over Storm's skull to steal the World Championship.

Since then, Storm has been on a mission to claw his way back to the headline spot, to seek retribution on his former friend and recapture the title that would validate his decade long TNA career.

46

HULK HOGAN

(🐦 @HULKHOGAN)

There is only one Hulk Hogan in professional wrestling and he calls TNA home. After a legendary career inside the squared circle, the 'Hulkster' now deals with most of his issues outside of the ring.

Having previously wrestled away ownership of TNA from Dixie Carter, Hulk finally saw the error of his ways following an epic confrontation with 'The Insane Icon' Sting at Bound for Glory.

In the spring of 2012, when Sting was looking to step down as general manager of Impact Wrestling, he argued that there was only one man who could replace him and steer the TNA ship forward. Though Dixie was hesitant at first given their past history, Hogan took the reins and became the General Manager to take TNA to the next level.

Knowing he still has some work to do to win back the trust of the Hulkamaniacs, Hogan has been a forward-thinking GM, introducing the 'Open Fight Night' where wrestlers from outside TNA have a shot at earning a TNA contract. With these and other changes in the pipeline, Impact Wrestling will be an exciting place to be with Hulk Hogan running wild.

Height: 6'7"
Weight: 302lbs
From: Venice Beach, California
Finishing Move: Atomic Leg Drop

KURT ANGLE

(🐦 @REALKurtAngle)

Still the only Olympic Gold medallist in wrestling history, Kurt Angle is the lynchpin of the TNA Heavyweight scene. As one of, if not the, most technically gifted wrestlers to ever enter a ring, Kurt Angle delivers a world-class performance whether the fans are cheering or booing him. It doesn't matter who steps into the ring with him, guaranteed. World class as a mat technician, given his gold medal level amateur background, Kurt is equally at home flying through the air and has often shown disregard for his own body, performing a moonsault from the top of a cage during his classic series of encounters with Jeff Hardy, which cost Angle the TNA Title.

Kurt redeemed himself with fans by saving his next opponent AJ Styles from an attack by Christopher Daniels and Kazarian. He now receives the adulation that his years of service deserve. Teaming with AJ to create a dream team, the duo defeated Daniels and Kazarian to lift the TNA Tag titles at Slammiversary this year.

Kurt Angle has beaten the best in the world and has a legacy in TNA few can match. As long as blood runs through his veins, Kurt Angle strives to add to his multiple title reigns. Kurt's non-stop, all-action style puts him at one with the TNA mantra and has made Angle one of the greatest of all time.

Height: 6'0"
Weight: 240lbs
From: Pittsburgh, Pennsylvania
Finishing Move: The Angle Slam

MR. ANDERSON
(@MRKenAnderson)

...ANDERSON!!!!! He is a fan favourite of the TNA audience who elicits excitement every time he steps through the curtain. No one in TNA talks the talk like Mr. Anderson. His mouth constantly gets him into trouble. He freely admits to being an '@$$hole' but has the ability to back up his talk. A former two-time TNA World Heavyweight Champion, by beating Jeff Hardy and Sting respectively in 2011, Mr. Anderson is never far from the spotlight.

Returning to Impact Wrestling after four months, Mr. Anderson seems to be taking a new direction. Forming alliances with first AJ Styles, Garett Bischoff and finally Jeff Hardy; could Anderson be auditioning a new permanent tag team partner to go after the tag straps?

Whether it's singles or tag gold that he is after, what's certain is you'll never forget the name Mr. Anderson. He'll tell it to you... TWICE.................ANDERSON!!!!!

Height: 6'2"
Weight: 243lbs
From: Green Bay, Wisconsin
Finishing Move: The Plunge

AJ STYLES

(🐦 @AJStylesOrg)

One of only two originals to have been with the company for the entire decade since TNA's inception in 2002, the 'Phenomenal' AJ Styles has been there, done that and got several of the t-shirts. It's no coincidence AJ is nicknamed 'phenomenal'. Anyone who has ever seen Styles perform in the ring would agree that he is THAT good. AJ is no one trick pony. A superstar in the air, on the mat and even outside the ring, there is not a style of wrestling that Styles is not at home with. Excelling at everything he does, AJ Styles earned his place as a TNA legend among the fans.

Having won every title there is to win in TNA multiple times, one wonders what is left for AJ Styles to achieve. The simple answer is AJ wants to be the best. He may have been side-tracked by his long-running feud with Christopher Daniels and Kazarian, but another run for the TNA World Title is never far from his mind and is never far from his future. Getting back to the top of the tree has to be AJ Styles' goal for 2013.

Height: 5'11"
Weight: 215lbs
From: Gainesville, Georgia
Finishing Move: The Styles Clash

DEVON

(@TestifyDevon)

A celebrated star of the tag team division with a place in wrestling history, thanks to his success as a member of Team 3D with Bully Ray, the powerful and charismatic New Yorker is always looking for ways to use that experience. Briefly forming a team with D'Angelo Dinero, Devon quickly found that repeating the tag success would not be an easy feat. Realising he could only rely on himself, Devon made the decision to go it alone.

'TESTIFY MY BROTHER, TESTIFY.' It was not only Bully Ray who made the successful transition to singles wrestler. Devon captured the TNA TV Title from Robbie E at Victory Road. The term 'baptism by fire' was never more apt than for the son of a pastor. After convincingly defeating Robbie E in a rematch at Lockdown, Devon was informed of one of several new innovations from TNA management; that the TV title must be defended every week on Impact Wrestling. Though a daunting prospect for a man still celebrating his first-ever singles title, Devon relished the challenge and took on all-comers thick and fast.

Can Devon continue to rise up the singles ranks? His many fans will hope so.

Height: 6'2"
Weight: 280lbs
From: New York, New York
Finishing Move: Spinebuster

KAZARIAN

(🐦 @FrankieKazarian)

The multi-time former X Division champion has been a standout performer in TNA for many years. But his actions in early 2012 left many fans confused. Turning on long-time friend AJ Styles, Kazarian formed a seemingly strange bedfellow's partnership with Christopher Daniels. Kazarian explained that the association was at first under duress to keep a secret regarding an alleged improper relationship between AJ and TNA President Dixie Carter from being exposed. When Kazarian learned of the secret, then the alliance with Daniels became mutual.

As a team, Kazarian and Daniels are now on the same page and the results proved as much when they defeated the popular combination of Magnus and Samoa Joe at Sacrifice 2012 to capture the TNA World Tag Team titles. Though AJ Styles enlisted the help of Kurt Angle to lift the straps from Kazarian and Daniels, the feud is far from over. There is a host of new challenges to contend with for the titles. Kazarian will have to rely on the speed, agility and mat skills that led him to become one of the pioneers of the X Division and one of the most respected superstars in TNA history, to enable the team to have continued success.

Height: 6'1"
Weight: 215lbs
From: Anaheim, California
Finishing Move: The Flux Capacitor

CRIMSON

(🐦 @OfficialCrimson)

Height: 6'6"
Weight: 252lbs
From: Brooklyn, New York
Finishing Move: Red Sky

Since Crimson set foot in TNA in December 2010, the 6'6" New Yorker became nearly unstoppable. No doubt he experienced his ups and downs, but as a singles competitor he was incredibly unbeaten for 18 months until he lost a hard-fought match to James Storm.

Prior to the defeat, Crimson was locked into an unlikely alliance with 'The Blueprint' Matt Morgan. After capturing the TNA Tag Team Titles from 'Mexican America' on Impact Wrestling, the two developed into an impressive unit with the size and strength needed to dominate the tag team ranks. For a time, they did. Then, four months later, cracks appeared to shatter the pair, and they lost the titles. Crimson turned on Morgan weeks later and revealed that they had merely been putting up with each other for the duration of their tandem.

No one has ever doubted the credentials of Crimson. Prior to his TNA life, Crimson served in the U.S. Army 101st Airborne Division and served two tours in Iraq. Now back walking to the beat of his own drum, Crimson looks to skyrocket to the top of TNA. Will Crimson recover from losing his undefeated streak and hitch a ride all the way to the TNA World title?

CAT GOT YOUR TONGUE?

Below are well-known wrestling phrases from the stars of TNA Impact Wrestling. Fans around the world scream the catchphrases with their favourite wrestlers on a nightly basis but can YOU finish these wrestling phrases.

1) SORRY ABOUT YOUR DAMN ▮▮▮▮▮▮▮▮▮
   (James Storm)

2) IT'S REAL! IT'S DAMN ▮▮▮▮▮▮▮
   (Kurt Angle)

3) OH MY BROTHER ▮▮▮▮▮▮▮▮
   (Devon)

4) IT'S ▮▮▮▮▮▮▮ FOLKS
   (Sting)

5) I'M SAMOA JOE AND I AM ▮▮▮ ▮▮▮▮▮
   (Samoa Joe)

6) IT ▮▮▮▮▮ TO BE ROODE
   (Bobby Roode)

7) WHATCHA GONNA DO ▮▮▮▮▮▮
   (Hulk Hogan)

8) THERE ARE TWO THINGS YOU CAN DO ABOUT IT. ▮▮▮▮▮ AND LIKE IT.
   (AJ Styles)

Answers on page 60-61

ROBBIE E

(🐦 @RobbieEIMPACT)

Sensing he needed some muscle for backup, Robbie E enlisted Rob Terry as his bodyguard in 2012 as 'Little Rob' joined forces with 'Big Rob'. Even more arrogant and conceited than before, there was barely enough room in the Impact Zone for Robbie E's ego.

Fresh from the Jersey Shore, spray tanned to the max, and sporting the gaudiest ring attire in TNA, you'd be forgiven for not taking Mr. E seriously. However, Robbie E proved on more than one occasion that he has the skills in the ring, having held both the X Division and TV titles. Since the TV title will now be defended every week on Impact Wrestling, Robbie E is desperate for the limelight. With 'Big Rob' to back him up, the future could still be bright for Robbie E.

Height: 5'11"
Weight: 201lbs
From: The Jersey Shore, New Jersey
Finishing Move: FTD (Fresh to Death)

CHRIS SABIN

As one half of the most dynamic and electrifying teams on the TNA roster, the Motor City Machine Guns, Chris Sabin returned to the Impact Zone with partner Alex Shelley in April, for the first time in a year. After both men had been sidelined with separate injuries at differing times during 2011 and 2012, fans were waiting with baited breath for the return of their heroes. With a strong youth following, the Motor City Machine Guns popularity had not waned during their hiatus. However, more than six weeks into their return, Shelley was gone and Sabin was left to fend on his own.

Going solo is nothing new for Sabin. For years, he has been a shining light in the X Division, and his legions of young fans have no doubt that he has the ability to challenge Austin Aries in time. His goal must be to add to his previous four reigns as X Division champion, which combined, lasted an amazing 338 days, ranking him No. 1 in TNA X Division history.

Whoever is in the ring with this aerial maestro better watch his back...and his front...and his sides, because Chris Sabin will hit you from all angles. With his sights locked firmly on capturing singles championships, fans had better strap themselves in for a helluva ride.

Height: 5'10"
Weight: 205lbs
From: Detroit, Michigan
Finishing Move: The Cradle Shock

AUSTIN ARIES

(@AustinAries)

On the 10th Anniversary of 9/11, at No Surrender, Austin Aries wrote his name in the TNA record books beating Brian Kendrick for his first X Division Championship. On March 12, 2012, his name was etched in stone as 'A-Double' overtook Christopher Daniels to have the longest single championship reign in X Division history.

Rebuilding the X Division in his own image is certainly what Austin Aries has been doing. Aries is a master tactician and an aerial wizard with a strong-style grappling game that can take an opponent off guard. For whomever stands opposite Aries in the Impact Zone, the challenge is more of a conundrum. How do you beat the man who can do it all?

His brash, in-your-face arrogance did not endear him to the Impact faithful at first, but with each passing five-star performance in the squared circle, the fans grew to respect him and then to love him. It was a respect and love he had earned through sheer hard work and one that he was happy to reciprocate.

Building a legacy as TNA X Division champion, Austin Aries battled anyone who put his name into the hat. Those who Aries defeated read like a who's who of the X Division. However, it was his victory over the much larger Bully Ray by submission that really turned heads. Is Aries about to break out of the X Division and rise to the top of TNA? It could be written in the stars for 'the greatest man that ever lived.'

Height: 5'9"
Weight: 210lbs
From: Milwaukee, Wisconsin
Finishing Move: The Brainbuster

BECOME A LIT

Sting has been entertaining fans for 25 years and one of the biggest reasons the kids love him is his awesome face paint. You can design your own Sting face masks on the outlines below. You can then cut

TLE STINGER

it out using the dotted line as a guide. Pull string through the holes at the sides to make your mask wearable. Become a little Stinger. (If necessary, ask an adult to help you cut your mask and make the eye holes).

QUIZ ANSWERS

P6-7 Guess Who?

 BOBBY ROODE (TNA HEAVYWEIGHT CHAMPIONSHIP)

 AUSTIN ARIES (TNA X DIVISION CHAMPIONSHIP)

 DEVON (TNA TV CHAMPIONSHIP)

 KAZARIAN & CHRISTOPHER DANIELS (TNA TAG TEAM CHAMPIONSHIPS)

 MISS TESSMACHER (TNA KNOCKOUTS CHAMPIONSHIP)

ODB & ERIC YOUNG (TNA KOCKOUTS TAG TEAM CHAMPIONSHIPS)

P17 Spot the Difference

P22 Crossword

P23 Wordsearch

P26-27 Calling the Moves with the Professor Quiz

1. KURT ANGLE (ANKLE LOCK)
2. EAT DEFEAT (GAIL KIM),
3. FIVE-STAR FROG SPLASH (ROB VAN DAM),
4. SCORPION DEATH LOCK (STING),

5. LAST CALL (JAMES STORM),
6. THE STROKE (JEFF JARRETT),
7. SWANTON (JEFF HARDY),
8. BORDER TOSS (HERNANDEZ),

P34-35 10 Year Quiz

1. THE ASYLUM
2. KEN SHAMROCK
3. SAMOA JOE
4. LONDON or WEMBLEY
5. HULK HOGAN, RIC FLAIR, JEFF HARDY
6. SEVEN
7. RAVEN
8. BOUND FOR GLORY

9. DON WEST
10. AMERICA'S MOST WANTED
11. KURT ANGLE, SAMOA JOE & ABYSS
12. CHALLENGE TV
13. AUSTIN STARR
14. TEAM 3D
15. JEFF JARRETT

SCORE RATING

20 Correct = You are an honouree inductee of the TNA Hall of Fame
15-19 = Hulk Hogan says you can be co-general manager of Impact wrestling.
10-14 = The decision is going to the Gut Check Panel...you just made it.
5-9 = Ouch, must do better. Kurt Angle is waiting to snap on the ankle lock.
0-4 = You need to go back and see the Professor, Mike Tenay.

P41 Maze

P45 Finish Him Wordsearch

P54 Cat Got Your Tongue

1. LUCK   4. SHOWTIME   7. BROTHER

WHERE'S HU

Hulk Hogan is hiding in th